ANCIENT
ROME

Tim Cooke

W
FRANKLIN WATTS
LONDON • SYDNEY

Published in Great Britain in 2018 by
The Watts Publishing Group

For Brown Bear Books Ltd:
Managing Editor: Tim Cooke
Children's Publisher: Anne O'Daly
Editorial Director: Lindsey Lowe
Design Manager: Keith Davis
Designer and Illustrator: Supriya Sahai
Picture Manager: Sophie Mortimer

Concept development: Square and Circus/
Brown Bear Books Ltd

ISBN: 978 1 4451 6189 1

Printed in Malaysia

Franklin Watts
An imprint of
Hachette Children's Group
Part of the Watts Publishing Group
Carmelite House
50 Victoria Embankment
London EC4Y 0DZ

An Hachette UK company
www.hachette.co.uk
www.franklinwatts.co.uk

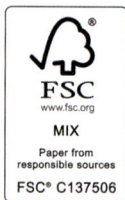

FSC
www.fsc.org
MIX
Paper from
responsible sources
FSC® C137506

CONTENTS

ANCIENT ROME

In the 700s BCE, Rome was founded as a farming settlement on the River Tiber in Italy. By the 400s BCE, it had grown into a city. The Romans began to conquer land in Italy and around the Mediterranean Sea.

ROMAN HISTORY

In its early days, Rome was a monarchy ruled by kings. Later it became a republic, ruled by a council called the Senate. In 27 BCE, Rome became an empire, ruled by emperors. At its height, the empire stretched from Spain in the west to Iraq in the east, and from Britain in the north to Egypt in the south. The Romans built cities throughout the empire modelled on Rome itself.

The Forum in the heart of Rome was an open area with many temples, public buildings and statues.

ROMAN EMPIRE IN CE 117

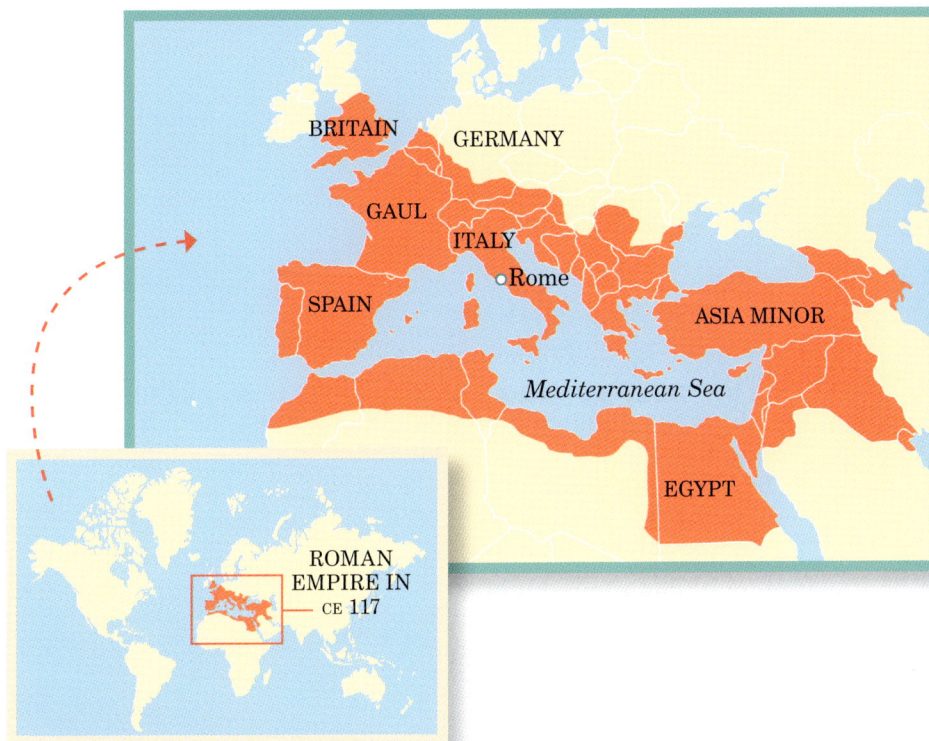

Everyone in the empire used Roman coins and obeyed Roman laws. Many spoke the Roman language, Latin. In return for their loyalty, the Romans gave all their subjects the right to call themselves citizens of Rome.

ARTEFACTS

The ancient Romans were skilled builders, craftspeople and artists. Many of the objects they made survive today, such as roads, mosaics and statues. One of the best ways to discover how the Romans lived and thought is by studying these artefacts. The objects enable us to step back into the world of the people who made them.

Julius Caesar was the last ruler of the Roman republic.

THE GROWTH OF ROME

Rome began in 753 BCE as a farming village near the River Tiber. The first buildings were on the Palatine Hill. By 200 BCE, about 310,000 people were living in Rome. By the start of the Roman Empire in 27 BCE, more than a million people lived there.

ITALY

Rome

Mediterranean Sea

The Forum was the main public part of the city. It was home to statues, temples and government buildings.

☞ THE FACTS

Rome was founded by a people called the Latins. They became known as Romans, after the city. The Romans were influenced by their neighbours, the Etruscans. The Etruscans controlled central Italy. They were skilled builders who taught the Romans to construct stone buildings using arches. The Romans were also influenced by Greeks. Some Greeks lived in settlements in southern Italy.

An aqueduct (see page 19) carried fresh water into the heart of the city from the surrounding countryside.

ROMULUS AND REMUS

The city's founding is described in a Roman legend about two brothers.

According to the story, Romulus and his twin brother, Remus, had been left to die as babies. They were found and fed by a female wolf and were later rescued by a shepherd. He and his wife brought the twins up as their own. As adults, Romulus and Remus decided to found a city. They fought over where to build it. Romulus killed Remus in an argument. He built a city on the Palatine Hill that was named after him, Rome.

The Colosseum was a huge arena for entertainments such as gladiator fights.

As this modern model of Rome in the first century BCE shows, most Romans lived in crowded apartment blocks.

This statue showing the wolf feeding Romulus and Remus stands on top of a pillar in Rome.

SENATORS AND ASSEMBLIES

In 509 BCE the Romans founded a republic. Roman citizens held meetings called assemblies. The assemblies voted for magistrates, who governed the city and its territory. The magistrates and assemblies were advised by a Senate of Roman nobles. The senators held the real power in Rome.

A senator makes a speech to members of the Senate. The Senate voted on important issues. Their decisions had a lot of power in ancient Rome.

THE TOGA

Roman men showed their social status in their togas.

A toga was a semicircular piece of cloth that was draped around the whole body. Only citizens were allowed to wear togas. The usual colour of the toga was white. Senators' togas had a broad border of red-purple. The colour was created with an expensive dye made from shellfish. For special occasions, senior magistrates and victorious generals wore togas that were dyed completely purple.

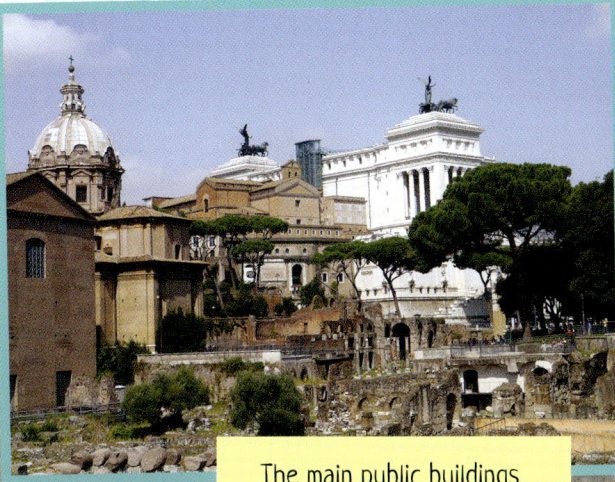

The main public buildings surrounded the Forum.

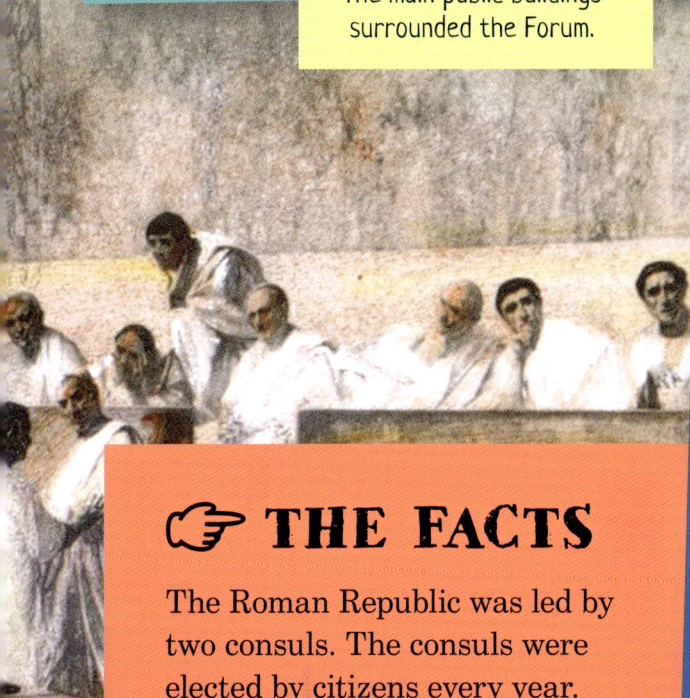

This statue of a man in a toga comes from the Diocletian Baths in Rome, built around CE 300.

👉 THE FACTS

The Roman Republic was led by two consuls. The consuls were elected by citizens every year. The consuls were helped by elected magistrates. The consuls and magistrates were advised by the senate. Senators came from Rome's oldest families. These so-called patricians had more rights than other Romans, called plebians (commoners). The plebians elected their own magistrates, called tribunes. Eventually, they gained the same rights as the patricians.

THE ROMAN EMPIRE

In 45 BCE, the general Julius Caesar took power in Rome as a dictator. Angry senators assassinated him the following year. A civil war broke out. It was won by Octavius, who was Caesar's nephew and adopted son. In 27 BCE, the Senate made him Augustus, which means emperor. This was the beginning of the Roman Empire.

These are the remains of the forum that Emperor Augustus built. He built a new forum because the original one was crowded with buildings.

EMPEROR AUGUSTUS

Augustus's 40-year reign was a time of peace and stability in the empire.

Augustus built roads and reformed the tax system to encourage trade. As Rome grew more wealthy, Augustus ordered the rebuilding of much of the city. He said that he found it a city of brick and left it a city of marble. He improved the army, which helped expand the empire in North Africa, Spain and Germany.

This replica of a statue discovered in 1863 shows Augustus as a powerful ruler of Rome.

Augustus's forum included this temple dedicated to Mars, the Roman god of war.

👉 THE FACTS

Emperors ruled Rome from 27 BCE until the fall of the empire in the west in CE 476. The emperors had great power. Although the Senate still existed, the emperor controlled it and could ignore its decisions. Some emperors chose their successors. Other emperors were chosen by the Roman army. Emperors came from all over the empire. Emperor Marcus Aurelius, for example (left), was from Spain.

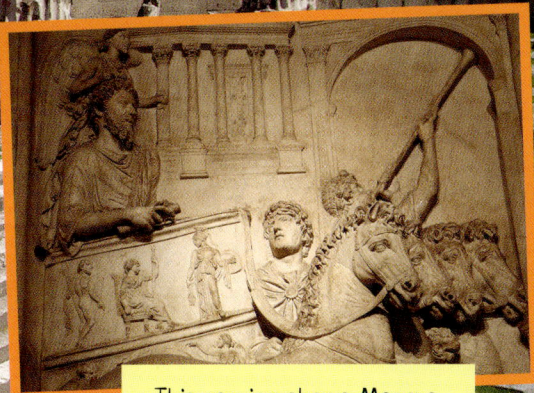

This carving shows Marcus Aurelius in a chariot taking part in a procession.

ROME'S ARMY

Rome's armies expanded the empire by conquering neighbouring peoples. As the Roman Empire grew larger, the army protected its borders from peoples who lived outside. Soldiers served in outposts from northern England to the deserts of Libya and the forests of the River Rhine in Germany.

☞ THE FACTS

- From the start of the Roman republic, Rome's armies gained new territories in a series of wars.
- To win control of the whole of Italy, Rome defeated Greek colonies in southern Italy.
- Rome fought three wars over the course of a century to defeat the North African city of Carthage. Rome gained control of North Africa and Spain.
- Between 215 and 148 BCE, Rome conquered Macedonia and Greece.
- By the late first century BCE, Rome had defeated the Gauls and conquered France.
- The Roman occupation of Britain began in CE 43.

SOLDIER'S HELMET

Rome had a professional and highly trained army. Soldiers signed up to serve in legions. Each legion had about 5,000 men.

A legion was divided into smaller groups, called centuries. A century had between 80 and 160 men. Centuries were commanded by veteran soldiers called centurions. Most legionaries were infantry, which meant they fought on foot rather than on horseback. Legionaries wore metal armour and a helmet, and carried a shield. They fought at close range with javelins, a short sword and a dagger.

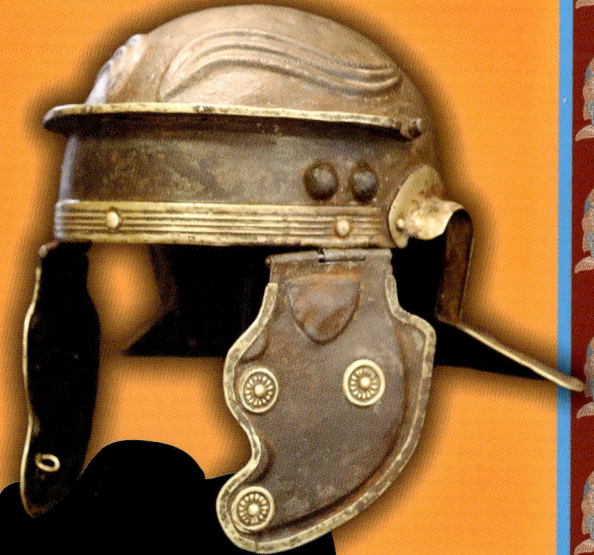

Emperor Hadrian built a wall to defend the edge of the empire in northern England.

The soldiers carry short swords for close-quarter fighting.

This stone carving shows Roman soldiers fighting against a people known as the Dacians, who lived in what is now the Balkans in southeastern Europe.

Roman helmets had flaps to protect the wearer's neck and cheeks.

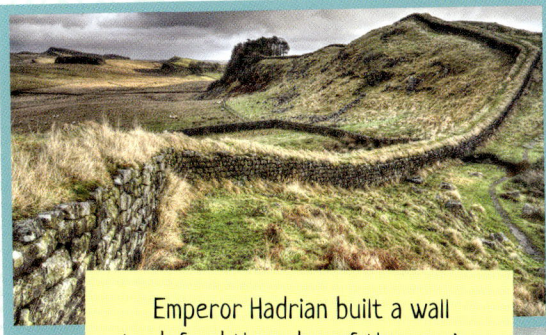

ROMAN GODS

The Romans worshipped many gods and goddesses. Each god was responsible for different aspects of life. The Romans included deities from many other places in the empire. Many Roman gods had originated in ancient Greece. The Romans simply gave them different names. Ares, the Greek god of war, became the Roman god Mars, for example.

☞ THE FACTS

- There were twelve main Roman gods, but there were also many less important local gods and goddesses.
- People had shrines in their homes, where they prayed to household gods called *lares*.
- Christianity began in Palestine (modern-day Middle East) when it was ruled by the Romans.
- Rome's emperors persecuted and killed early Christians for their beliefs.

ALTAR

The twelve main Roman gods and goddesses each had their own responsibilities:

Jupiter – king of the gods
Juno – queen of the gods
Neptune – god of the sea
Pluto – god of the Underworld
Vesta – goddess of the home
Minerva – goddess of wisdom
Diana – goddess of the hunt
Apollo – god of light and music
Venus – goddess of beauty
Vulcan – god of fire and ironworking
Mars – god of war
Mercury – messenger of the gods

Minerva was the goddess of wisdom and was Jupiter's daughter. She was a version of the Greek goddess Athena.

The Pantheon in Rome was the only temple dedicated to all the Roman gods and goddesses. It was built in CE 126.

This altar showing the twelve main gods was made in the first century CE. It was found in 1792 in Gabii, Italy.

CITIES

The Romans founded cities throughout their empire. All the cities had similar buildings. Cities usually included a forum. This open space was home to temples, courts and government buildings. Towns also had public baths and places for entertainment.

ITALY
Rome
Pompeii
Mediterranean Sea

☞ THE FACTS

- Wealthy people lived in large villas. Poorer people lived in crowded apartment blocks.
- Traders lived above their workshops and shops.
- Different professions lived in their own parts of the city.
- Aqueducts brought fresh water into cities for drinking and for washing.
- The water was used for drinking fountains and for public baths.
- People visited the baths often to get clean and meet their friends.

This street in Pompeii had stepping stones so people could cross without getting their feet dirty or wet.

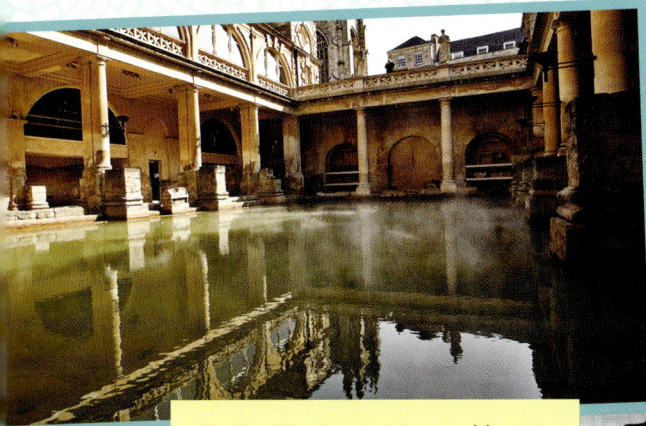
All Roman towns featured baths, like this one at Bath in England.

DOG MOSAIC

This mosaic was an ancient 'beware of the dog' sign!

It was discovered in a house in Pompeii, a town near the coast of southern Italy. In CE 79, Pompeii was buried by ash after the eruption of the nearby volcano, Vesuvius. The ash and lava preserved the town and its buildings. Archaeologists have cleared much of the buried town. They found houses with tables set for meals, as well as vegetable gardens and graffiti written on walls. This kind of evidence tells them a lot about how ordinary Romans lived.

The streets were lined by houses with workshops or shops at the front.

Pompeiians decorated the walls of their homes with mosaics and murals.

ROADS AND ENGINEERING

The Romans built a network of roads to connect the towns and cities of the empire. The roads allowed soldiers to move around rapidly in case of trouble. Roads also made it easier for traders to transport goods. Many kilometres of Roman road are still in use.

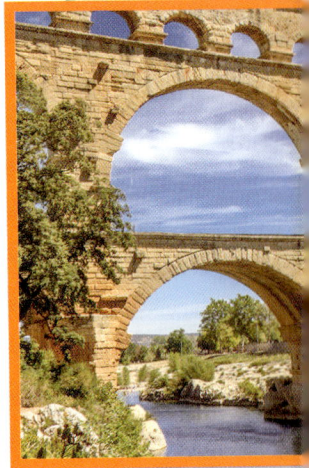

About 85,000 km of Roman roads were paved with stone blocks.

A Roman road in the Gredos mountains in Spain.

☞ THE FACTS

- The first roads were built radiating out from Rome across Italy.
- At the height of the empire, there were 400,000 km of roads.
- The roads were built as straight as possible to keep journeys short.

- The roads were built by soldiers, who smoothed a roadway and dug ditches along the edges for drainage. The road was covered with sand, then flattened or paved with stone blocks.

GROMA

The Romans were expert engineers and builders. Many structures they built are still standing.

Surveyors travelled with the army. They laid out the routes of new roads. When the soldiers built a camp, surveyors laid out regular blocks and streets inside a defensive wooden wall. More permanent outposts were built from stone, such as the forts along Hadrian's Wall. One of the Romans' greatest feats of engineering was their water system. Aqueducts carried fresh water many kilometres from the countryside into the cities. In the cities, water flowed through underground tunnels and pipes.

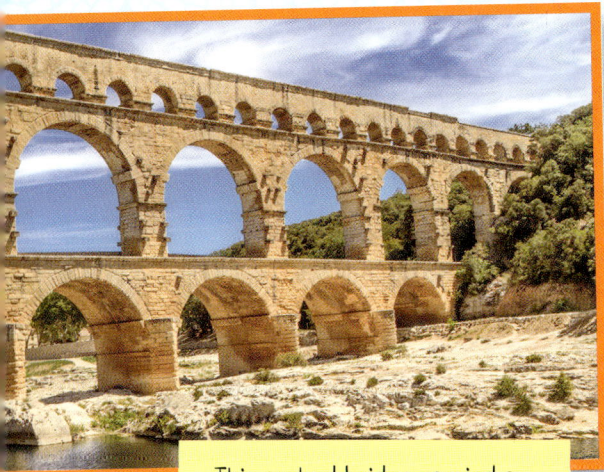

This arched bridge carried an aqueduct over a river in southern France.

Surveyors used a *groma* to measure the land. Hanging weights helped ensure the *groma* was upright.

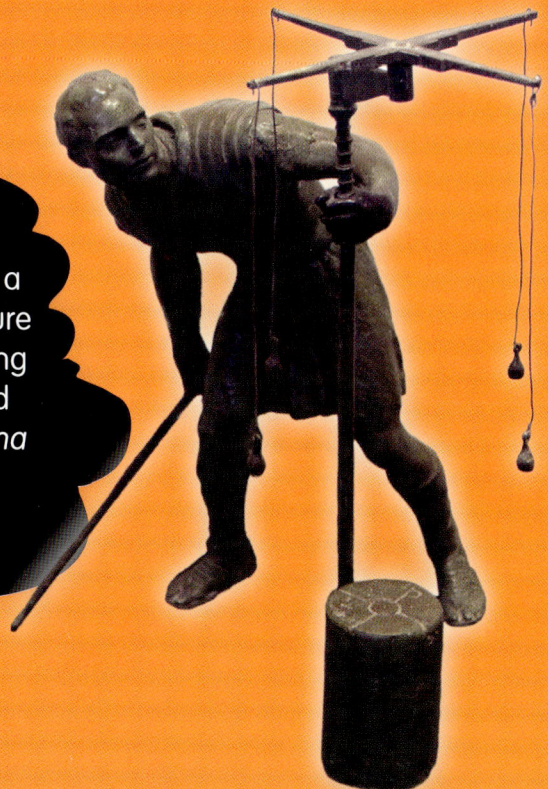

TRADE

The Romans built roads and harbours. They encouraged merchants to travel by land and sea. Goods from around the world arrived in major Roman cities. Rome had its own thriving port at Ostia. Goods were unloaded at Ostia then brought 30 km up the River Tiber to Rome.

ITALY

Rome

Ostia

Mediterranean Sea

☞ THE FACTS

The Roman emperors encouraged trade, because it helped them raise taxes. The empire introduced standard coinage, and made sure that weights and measures were the same throughout the empire. Trade routes led as far east as China and India, into North Africa and the Middle East and throughout Europe. Roman merchants imported silk from China, spices from India, cotton from Egypt and tin from Britain.

In the CE 100s and 200s, Ostia had up to 100,000 inhabitants.

ROMAN COINS

From the 400s BCE the Romans made coins of various sizes in gold, silver, bronze and copper.

The coins were used throughout the Roman territories. Early coins sometimes carried the image of an important ancestor of the Romans. Julius Caesar was the first ruler to put his own portrait on coins. After him, all emperors did the same. Coins became an important way to show the strength of the emperor and the empire. For some citizens, coins were the only connection they had with the emperor.

These Roman coins show Emperor Vespasian (right) and Julia Domna (below), wife of Emperor Lucius Septimius Severus.

The ruins of warehouses and granaries (where grain was stored) still stand in Ostia.

Imports arrived in Ostia from throughout the Mediterranean. Among the most important was grain from North Africa.

ENTERTAINMENT

Although the Roman Empire and its rulers grew rich, many ordinary Romans were poor. The emperors were afraid that their subjects might rise up against them. One way they tried to keep the population happy was by putting on free entertainments in arenas such as the Colosseum in Rome.

The oval-shaped Colosseum was surrounded by banks of seating for spectators.

☞ THE FACTS

- The Colosseum was built in Rome between CE 70 and 80.
- It could hold up to 80,000 spectators.
- The Colosseum could be flooded to re-enact naval battles.
- The Romans enjoyed watching fights between gladiators and between men and wild animals. Horse and chariot racing were popular, too. Romans also enjoyed watching public executions.

GLADIATORS

One of the most popular forms of entertainment was gladiator combat.

Gladiators were often slaves or prisoners of war. They were trained to fight one another to the death with swords, nets and other weapons. In so-called beast shows, gladiators also fought against dangerous wild animals, such as lions. Gladiator fights were big business. Successful gladiators became famous heroes. They fought in amphitheatres throughout the Roman world.

This carving of two gladiators dates from the first to third centuries CE. It was found in Rome in 1880.

At the end of a gladiator fight, the audience shouted for the defeated opponent to live or die. The emperor made the final decision.

THE END OF THE EMPIRE

By CE 285, the Roman Empire was too big to govern. It split into two regions. The Western Empire was ruled from Rome. The Eastern Empire was ruled from Byzantium (now Istanbul in modern-day Turkey). In 330, the Emperor Constantine renamed Byzantium Constantinople.

This mosaic of Constantine was made in the Byzantine Empire in around 1000.

☞ THE FACTS

- The Empire in the West was overthrown by Germanic warriors from eastern Europe in 476.
- The Empire in the East survived and became known as the Byzantine Empire. It lasted until 1453.
- In Europe, the fall of Rome led to a rise in warfare and a decline in trade, scholarship and building. This marked the start of the Middle Ages.
- The Roman Catholic Church was the main religion in Europe. It was based in Rome. It kept alive the Roman language, Latin.

Constantinople was protected by huge Roman walls.

HEAD OF CONSTANTINE

Constantine was an army officer, whose men proclaimed him emperor in 306.

He fought against his fellow emperors to become sole ruler by 324. Constantine converted to Christianity, and made it legal to follow Christianity within the empire. He reformed the Roman army to resist invasions by peoples living on the borders of the empire, such as the Franks and Goths. In 476, however, German barbarians led by Odoacer overthrew Romulus, the last Roman emperor in the West.

Rome

Constantinople

ASIA MINOR

Mediterranean Sea

EGYPT

WESTERN ROMAN EMPIRE

BYZANTINE EMPIRE

Constantine presents a model of Constantinople as a gift to Mary and Jesus.

This carved head was part of a seated statue of Constantine in Rome that was around 12 metres tall.

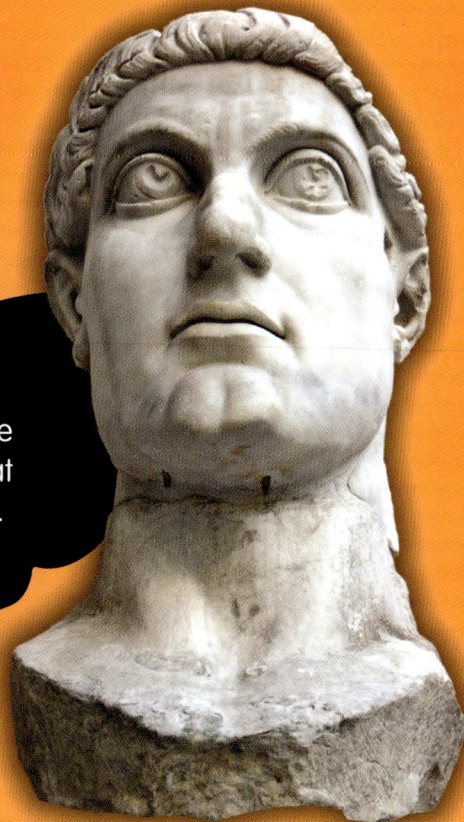

CERES AND PROSERPINA

Just as artefacts tell us a lot about cultures from the past, the stories people told reveal what they thought about their world. Ancient cultures used myths to explain their beliefs. This Roman myth told how the seasons began.

Ceres was an important goddess, as the Romans depended on the fruitfulness of agriculture.

Ceres, the goddess of fruitfulness, was a sister of Jupiter, king of the gods, Neptune, god of the sea, and Pluto, god of the Underworld. Ceres worried that the other gods would try to pursue her beautiful daughter, Proserpina. She tried to hide Proserpina by sending her to the island of Sicily.

One day, Proserpina went for a walk to pick flowers in the fields. While she was walking, she was spotted by her uncle, Pluto. Pluto rose up from the Underworld in his chariot. He seized Proserpina, and carried her off to his kingdom, where he made her his queen.

When Ceres found out that her daughter had disappeared, she was heartbroken. She left her home on Mount Olympus to search the world for Proserpina.

Because Ceres neglected her duties, the earth was no longer fruitful. Crops dried up and died. Animals gave no milk and had no young. Soon, people began to die of hunger.

Jupiter was troubled. He learned that Proserpina was with Pluto. He tried to persuade Ceres to give up her search to end all the suffering. Ceres refused to return to her duties until she had her daughter back.

Jupiter now ordered Pluto to return Prosperpina to her mother. Although Pluto argued, he had no choice but to agree. However, now Jupiter and Ceres learned that Prosperina had eaten pomegranate seeds at her wedding feast. Pomegranate was the fruit of the dead. Proserpina belonged to the Underworld for ever.

Jupiter arranged a compromise. He suggested that Prosperpina should spend half of each year on earth and the other half in the Underworld. That is how the seasons began. For the six months Proserpina spends with her mother, plants flower and yield fruit and seeds. For the six months she spends in the Underworld, plants wither and die through the winter.

TIMELINE OF ANCIENT ROME

146 BCE
The third Punic War results in victory for Rome.

753 BCE
Traditional date of Rome's founding by Romulus.

45 BCE
Julius Caesar makes himself dictator for life.

CE 80
The Colosseum is built in Rome.

700s BCE

100s BCE

CE 0

509 BCE
The Romans depose their king and establish a republic.

44 BCE
Julius Caesar is assassinated.

CE 64
Much of Rome is destroyed in a huge fire during the reign of Emperor Nero.

264 BCE
The first of three Punic Wars begin in which Rome fights the city of Carthage.

27 BCE
At the end of the civil wars that follow the death of Caesar, Octavius becomes the first emperor under the name Augustus.

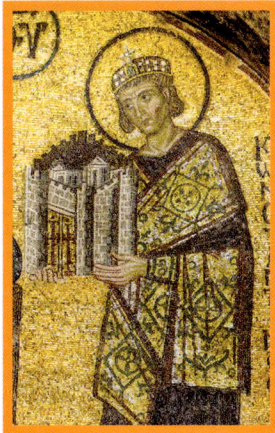

CE 395
The Roman Empire splits into western and eastern parts.

CE 306
Constantine becomes emperor of Rome.

CE 476
The last Roman emperor is overthrown, marking the end of the Western Empire.

CE 330
Constantine moves his capital to Byzantium, which he renames Constantinople.

CE 117
The empire reaches its greatest extent, under Emperor Trajan.

CE 100s	CE 300s	CE 400s	CE 1400s

CE 121
Emperor Hadrian builds a wall along the empire's border in Britain.

CE 380
Christianity becomes the official religion of the Roman Empire.

CE 1453
Muslim Turks called the Ottomans conquer Constantinople, ending the Eastern Empire.

CE 313
Constantine issues the Edict of Milan, permitting Christianity in the empire.

CE 410
A people named the Visigoths sack, or plunder, the city of Rome.

GLOSSARY

amphitheatre a circular or oval stadium for staging entertainments or sports

aqueduct an artificial channel that carries water over long distances

artefacts objects that have been made by people

assassinated murdered for a political reason

barbarians the Roman name for people who were not Roman citizens

civil war a conflict between two groups from the same country

colonies settlements or regions governed by a different country

consul one of the two chief magistrates elected every year to rule the Roman republic

dictator a ruler with absolute authority

emperor in ancient Rome, a king-like ruler with supreme power

forum a public square or marketplace used for carrying out public administration

gladiator a man trained to fight with weapons against other gladiators or wild animals

groma an instrument used by surveyors to measure straight lines

imported brought from other countries

infantry soldiers who fight on foot

javelins light spears thrown as weapons

legion the main fighting unit in the Roman army

magistrate an official responsible for upholding laws and holding courts

monarchy a form of government in which the ruler is a king or a queen

mosaic a picture or pattern made up from small pieces of stone or glass

murals pictures or designs that are painted directly onto walls

persecuted treated a group of people unfairly because of their beliefs, race or opinions

republic a state that is governed by representatives elected by the people rather than by a monarch

sacked attacked a city, destroying buildings and stealing valuables

surveyor a person who marks where buildings or roads are to be built

Underworld the place where ancient Romans believed people went after death

FURTHER RESOURCES

Books

Ancient Rome, Eyewitness
(Dorling Kindersley, 2016)

At Home with the Ancient Romans, Tim Cooke
(Wayland, 2016)

Meet the Ancient Romans, Alex Woolf
(Franklin Watts, 2016)

Romans, Moira Butterfield
(Franklin Watts, 2014)

Romans, Sir Tony Robinson
(Macmillan Children's Books, 2012)

Websites

www.bbc.co.uk/education/topics/zwmpfg8
Learner guides and video clips about life in the Roman Empire.

www.bbc.co.uk/history/historic_figures/caesar_julius.shtml
Find out about the influential life of Julius Caesar and
the end of the Roman Republic.

www.primaryhomeworkhelp.co.uk/Romans.html
This site has information to help with homework
and projects about the ancient Romans.

INDEX

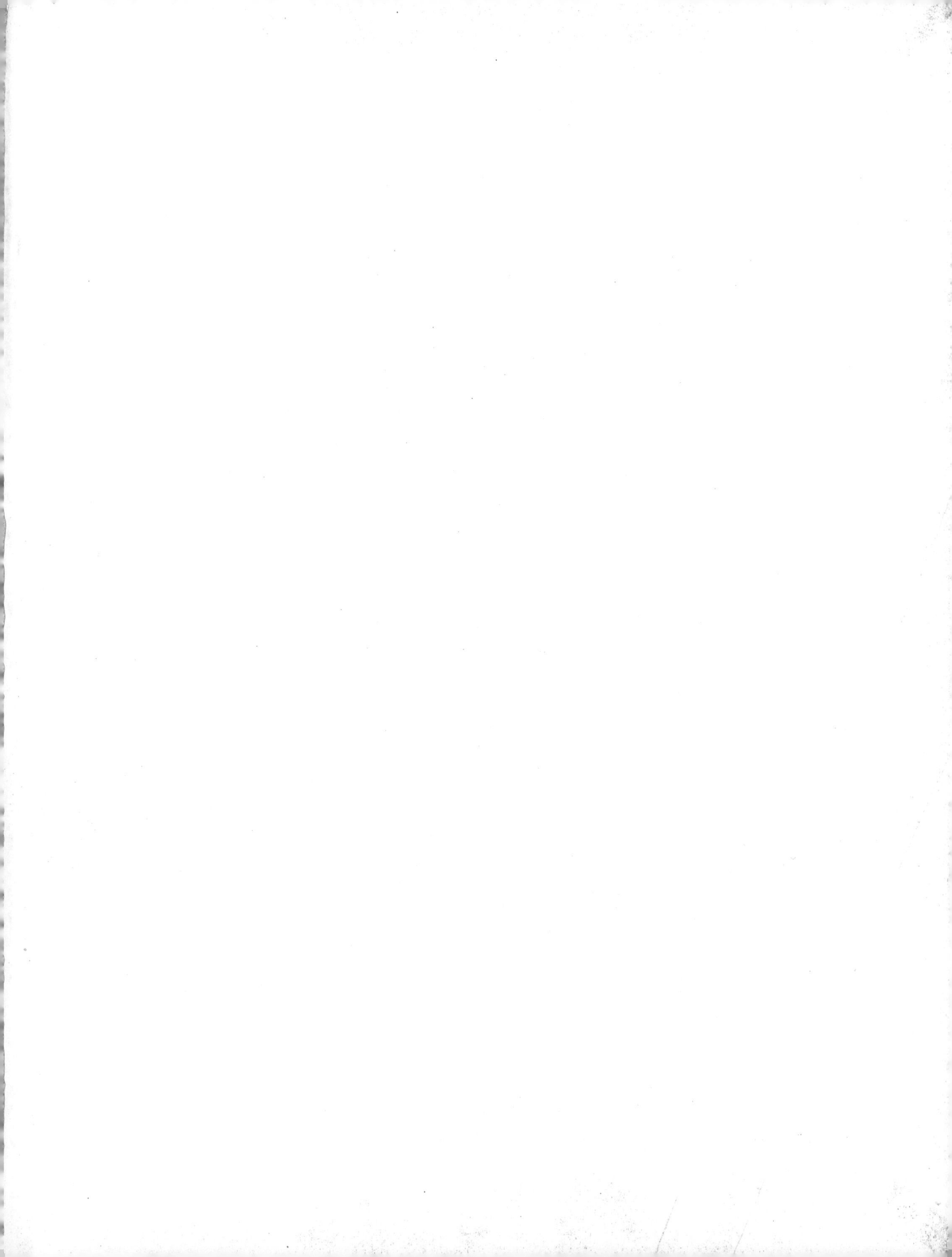